Michael Winters was born and raised in New Jersey and is the father of three beautiful daughters, Ivy, Meadow, and Violet. He can often be found creating stories, songs, jokes, and games with children. *Words, Werds, W-oh-er-dz* is Michael's first children's book. It's a fun and humorous journey into the numerous, diverse, and unique varieties of words we have the privilege of exploring.

Long · Left · Up · Big
Short · Right · Down · Small

For
Four · To
Fore · Too
 · Two

WORDS

Rhyme
Time

High
Low

WERDS

Run
Fun

I
eye

W-OH-
ER-DZ

Yummy
Tummy

by
buy
bye

Austin Macauley Publishers
LONDON · CAMBRIDGE · NEW YORK · SHARJAH

Cartoons
Car tunes · And · So · Much · More!

by:
Michael
Winters

Copyright © **Michael Winters** 2023

The right of **Michael Winters** to be identified as author of this work has been asserted by the author in accordance with sections 77 and 78 of the Copyright, Designs and Patents Act 1988.

All rights reserved. No part of this publication may be reproduced, stored in a retrieval system, or transmitted in any form or by any means, electronic, mechanical, photocopying, recording, or otherwise, without the prior permission of the publishers.

Any person who commits any unauthorised act in relation to this publication may be liable to criminal prosecution and civil claims for damages.

A CIP catalogue record for this title is available from the British Library.

ISBN 9781035807819 (Paperback)
ISBN 9781035807826 (ePub e-book)

www.austinmacauley.com

First Published 2023
Austin Macauley Publishers Ltd®
1 Canada Square
Canary Wharf
London
E14 5AA

For my three perfect little treasures, Ivy, Meadow, and Violet. You inspire me to create new things every day. This book is for you.

A special thank you to my family and friends for always building me up and supporting me throughout this exciting journey.

Words can be funny. Funny. That's a funny word. It's like your knee is having fun. How do knees have fun? Do they talk to each other when you're asleep? Can they breathe when you're wearing pants? Do they get cold when you wear shorts? Shorts... Also, kind of weird. If shorts are shorts, why aren't pants called longs?

FUNNY = FUN-KNEES

Then you have T-shirts. I get it; it's shaped like a "T". But if it has long sleeves, is it an "uppercase T"-shirt? We park in the driveway and drive on the parkway. Highways aren't high. Anyway, why do we have highways but don't have low-ways? And what about the word cartoon? I love cartoons. But you would think they should all be about cars playing tunes.

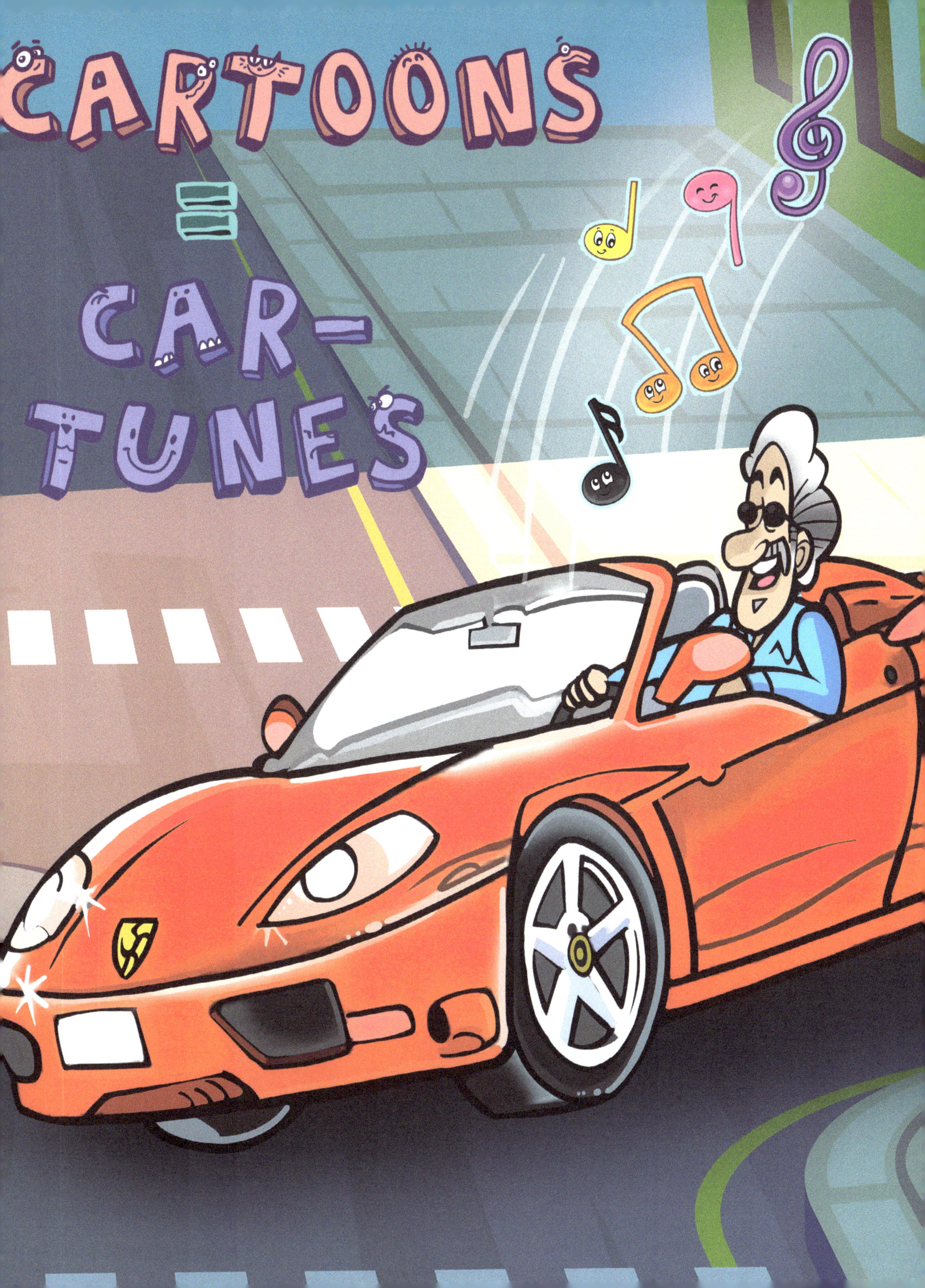
CARTOONS
=
CAR-
TUNES

Words can be confusing too. One deer is a deer. But two or more... are still deer; however, a mouse is a mouse and two would be mice. One fish is a fish and two fish are also fish. And if you play a game with dice, one is called a die!

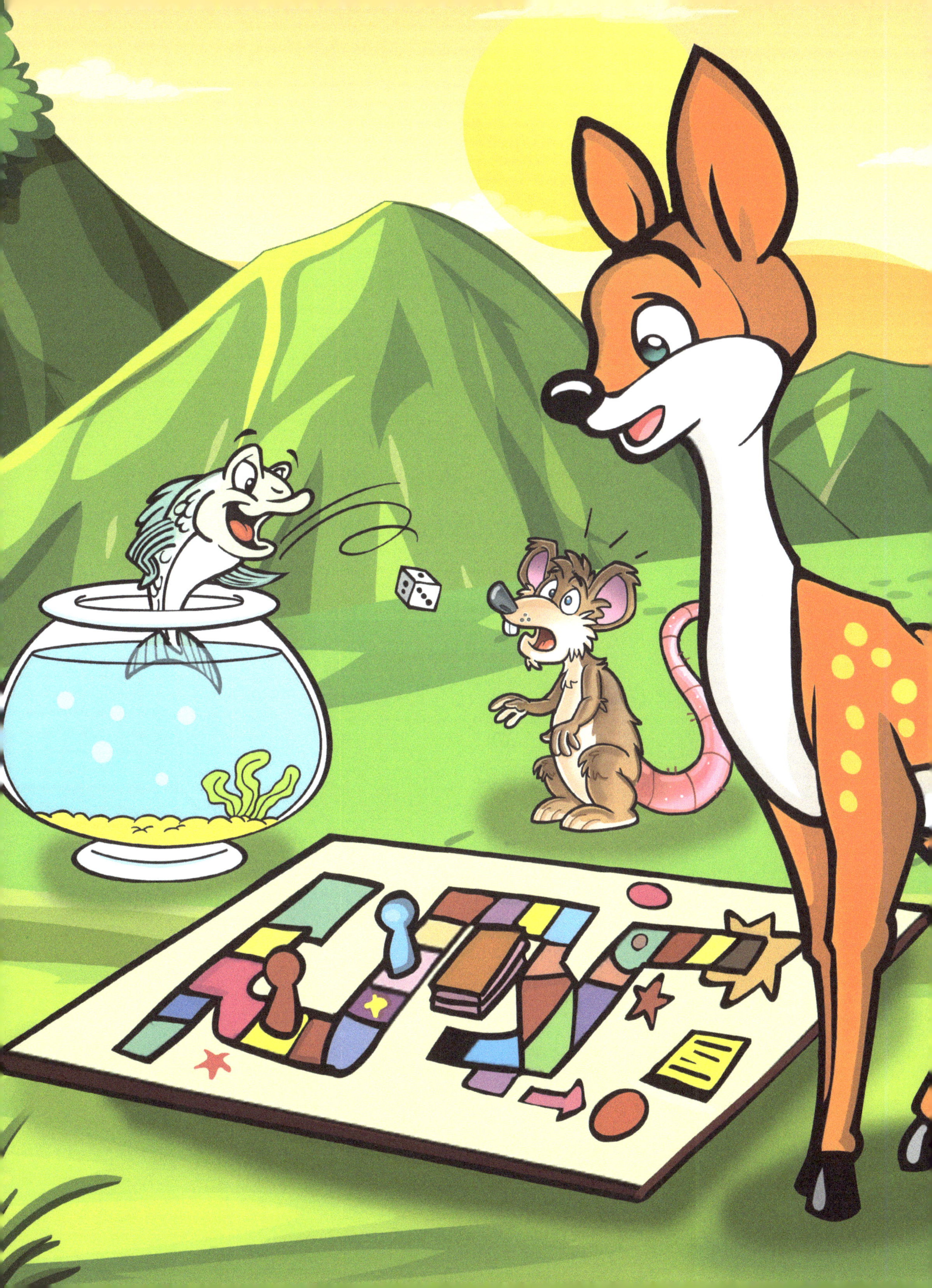

We have three ways to say "to, too and two".

And three ways to say "for, four, and fore".

Then there's need, knead and kneed. You "need" to "knead" flour to make your bread. You "kneed" on the ground to pick a flower for a friend.

TO, TOO, TWO / FOR, FOUR, FORE / KNEAD, KNEED, NEED, ETC

You use your eyes to "see" the "sea". You can "write" the word "right". But you can't left the word write. You can say that you "rode" on the "road". Or that you "ate", "eight" slices of pizza. Now that would be a lot. But it sure "beats" eating "beets".

You can go to the mall that's "by" your home and "buy" a toy and say "bye" to the girl working in the store. You can say "hi" to a bird that's "high" in the tree. Or put a "whole" bunch of carrots in the "hole" for a rabbit.

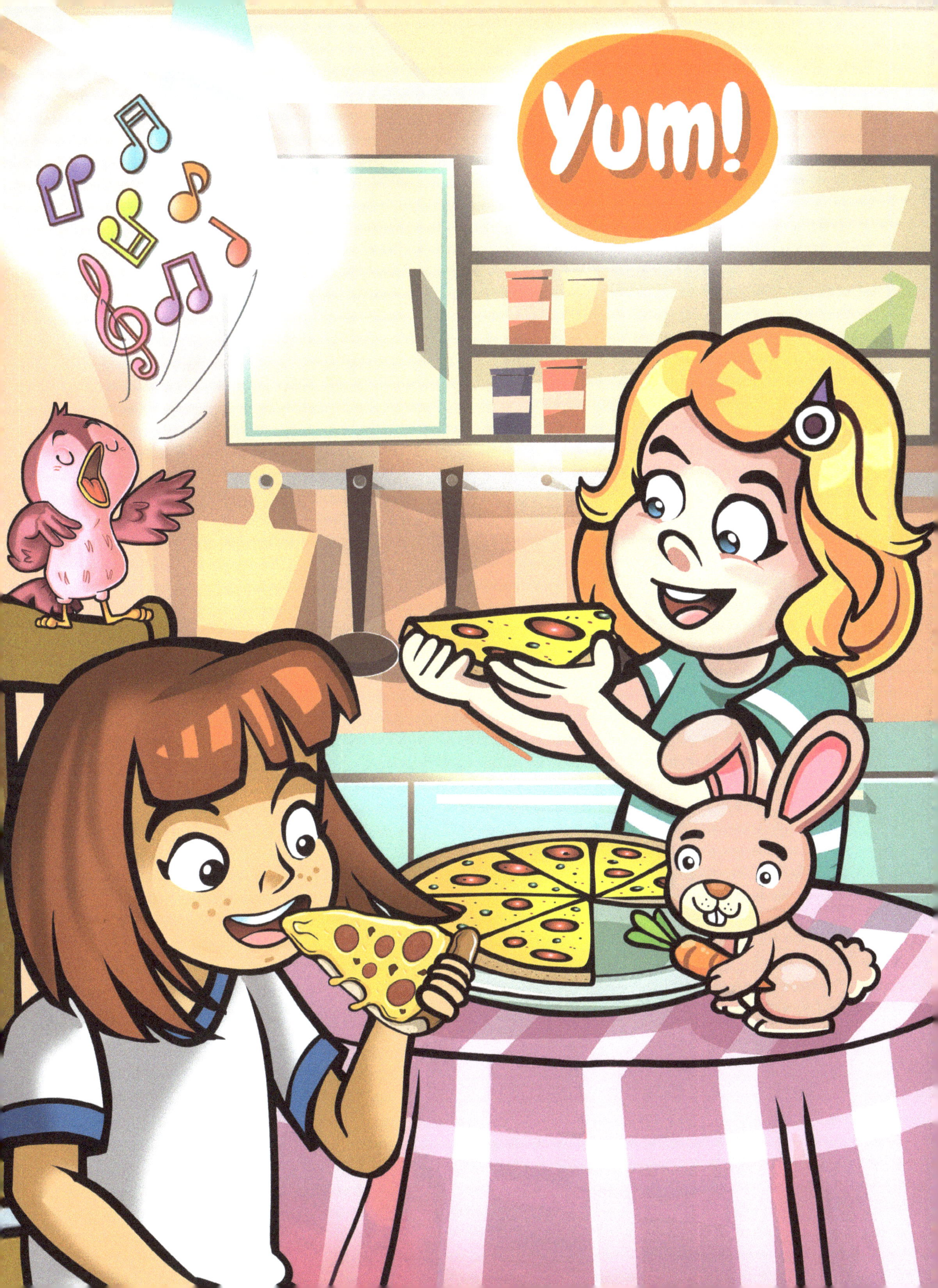
Yum!

If you're rich, you may say my "maid", "made" my bed. If you play a game and got a trophy, you can say, I "won" "one"! You can be calm and at "peace". You can eat cake, but just a "piece". A doctor must have "patience" with his or her "patients". You can write a little "tale" about a dragon with a little "tail". And if you like a nice salad, you can say, "Dad, "let us" have "lettuce"!" Anyway, I think you get the point.

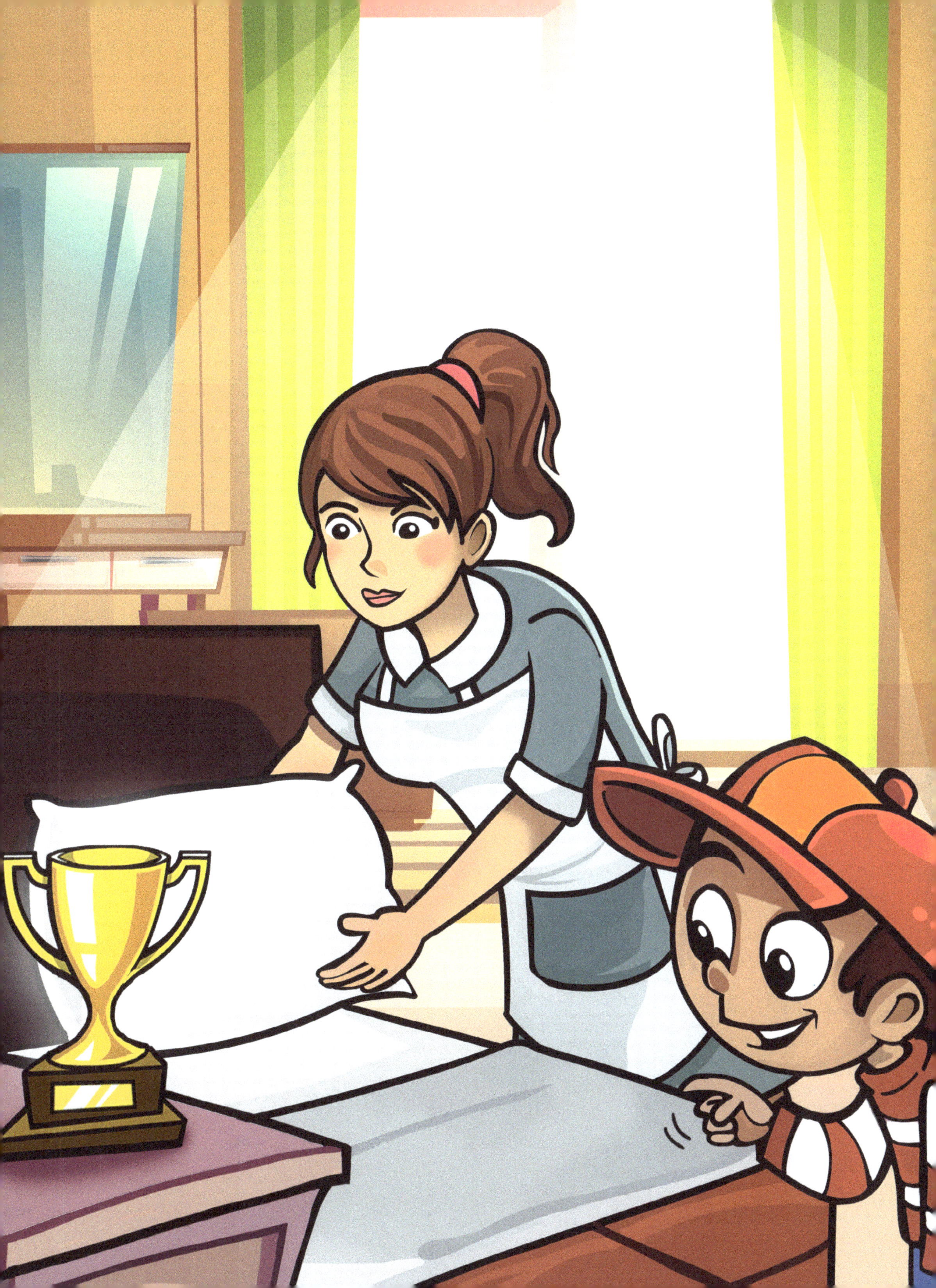

Yes, words can be tricky, too. Some letters are silent like the letter "h" in the word ghost. You would think it should sound like gu-host.

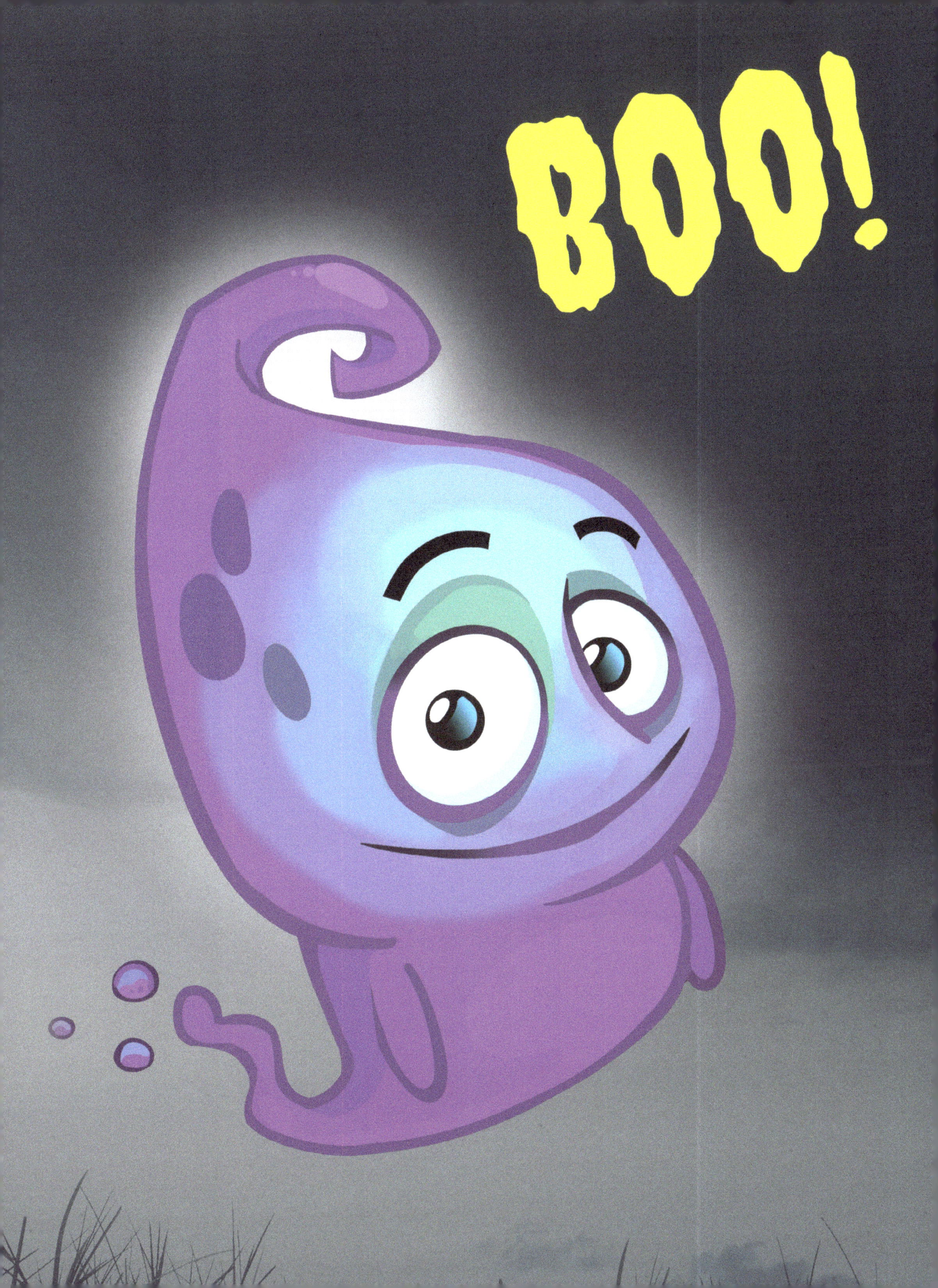
BOO!

Instead of kneeling on the ground, you would be ku-neeling. If you were full, you would say "I had e-nug-hu instead of enough." If someone asks if you want a piece of cake, you'd say, "Yes I woo-l-d" instead of would. When you introduce yourself to someone new, you'd say, "My nam-e is eye-vee-ya or me-ah-duh-ow-wa or v-eye-oh-let" Instead of Ivy, Meadow, or Violet.

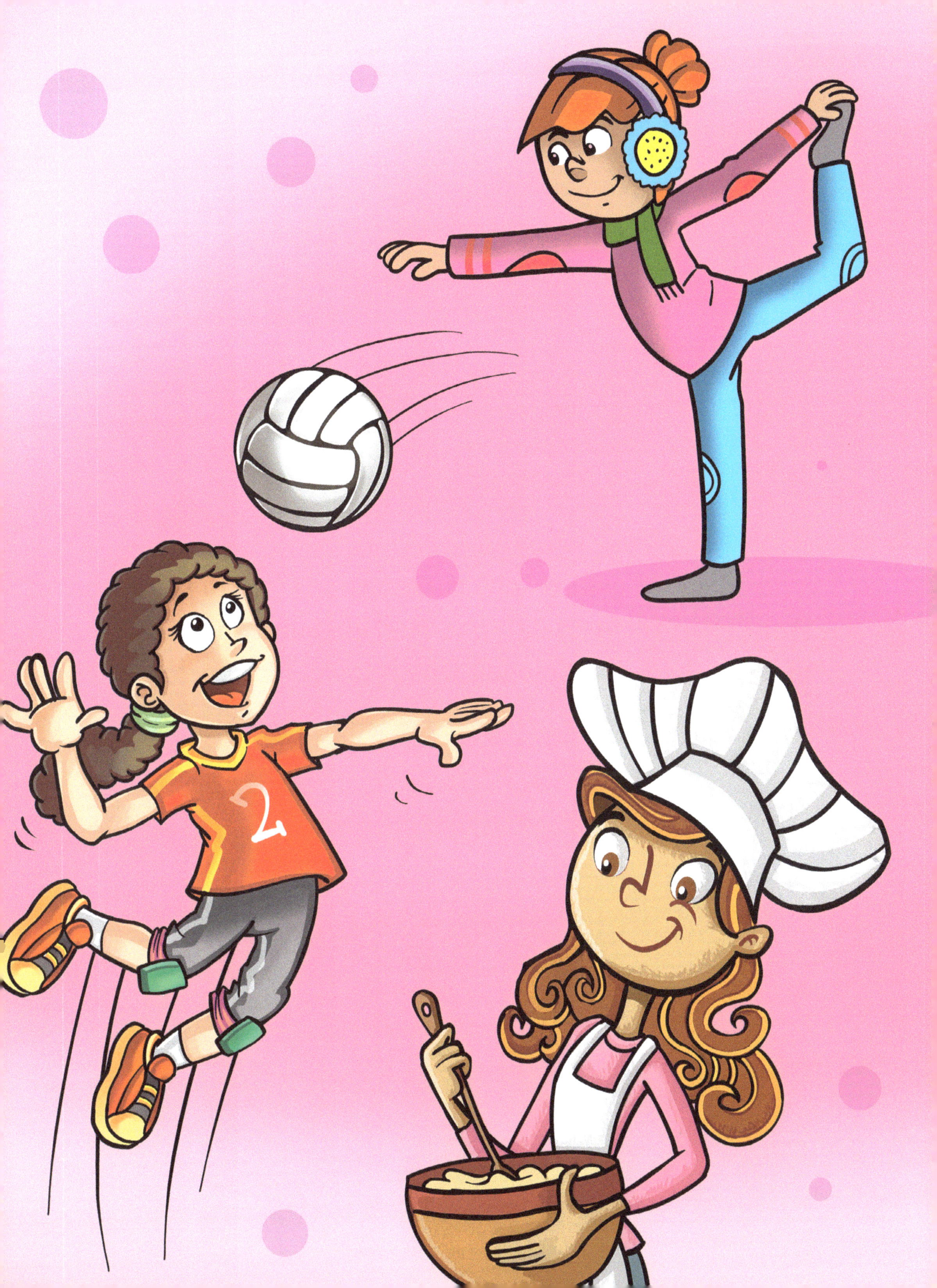

What a world where "ph" makes the "f" sound. Put the letter "p" in front of "s", and it still sounds like "s". Then you have the word Colonel, which looks like Co-lon-el but sounds like kernel which is also a word!

P H

You have biiiiiiig words and smmmmmmall words. You can go from one of the smallest words, "I", (which means you) to the biggest word in the English language, Pneumonoultramicroscopicsilicovolcanoniosis, which is a disease from inhaling a certain kind of dust... Then there is the word, "a" (which you pronounce uh), or the word, antidisestablishmentarianism, which has to do with the church.

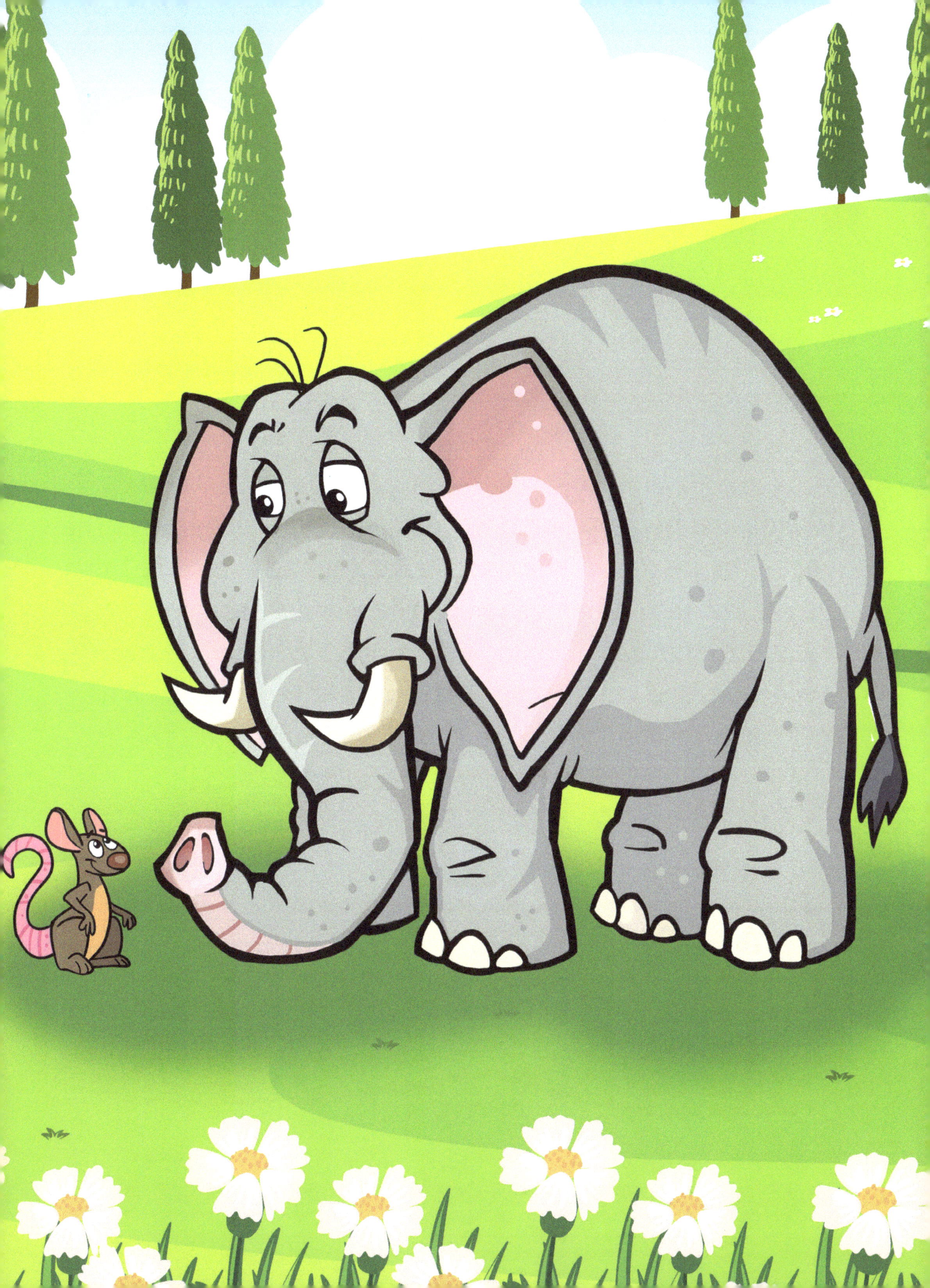

Words can be fun. Some words sound like the things they are. For instance, the word buzz sounds like something buzzzzz-ing. When you hear the word splash, you can't help but think of jumping into a pool. When you have the hiccups, and you hiccup it sounds like a... hiccup. When your mom or dad is cooking something yummy on the stove, you hear it sizzzzzzzle.

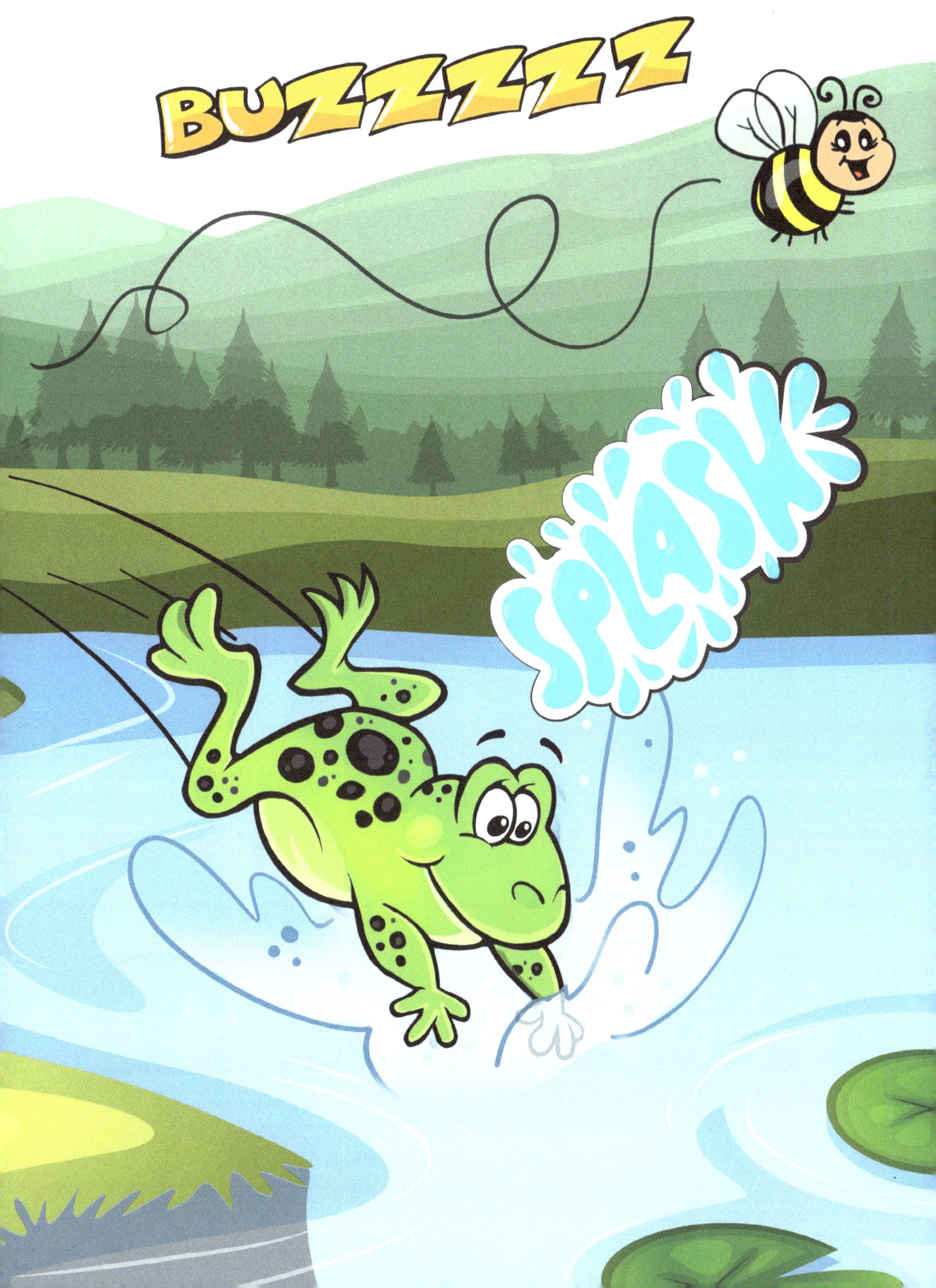
BUZZZZZZ
SPLASH

There are even a few words that are spelled the same forward and backward. Some of them are short like nun, wow, pop, bib, sis, mom, and dad. Some are a bit longer like refer, radar, madam, and even longer like racecar, redder, and repaper.

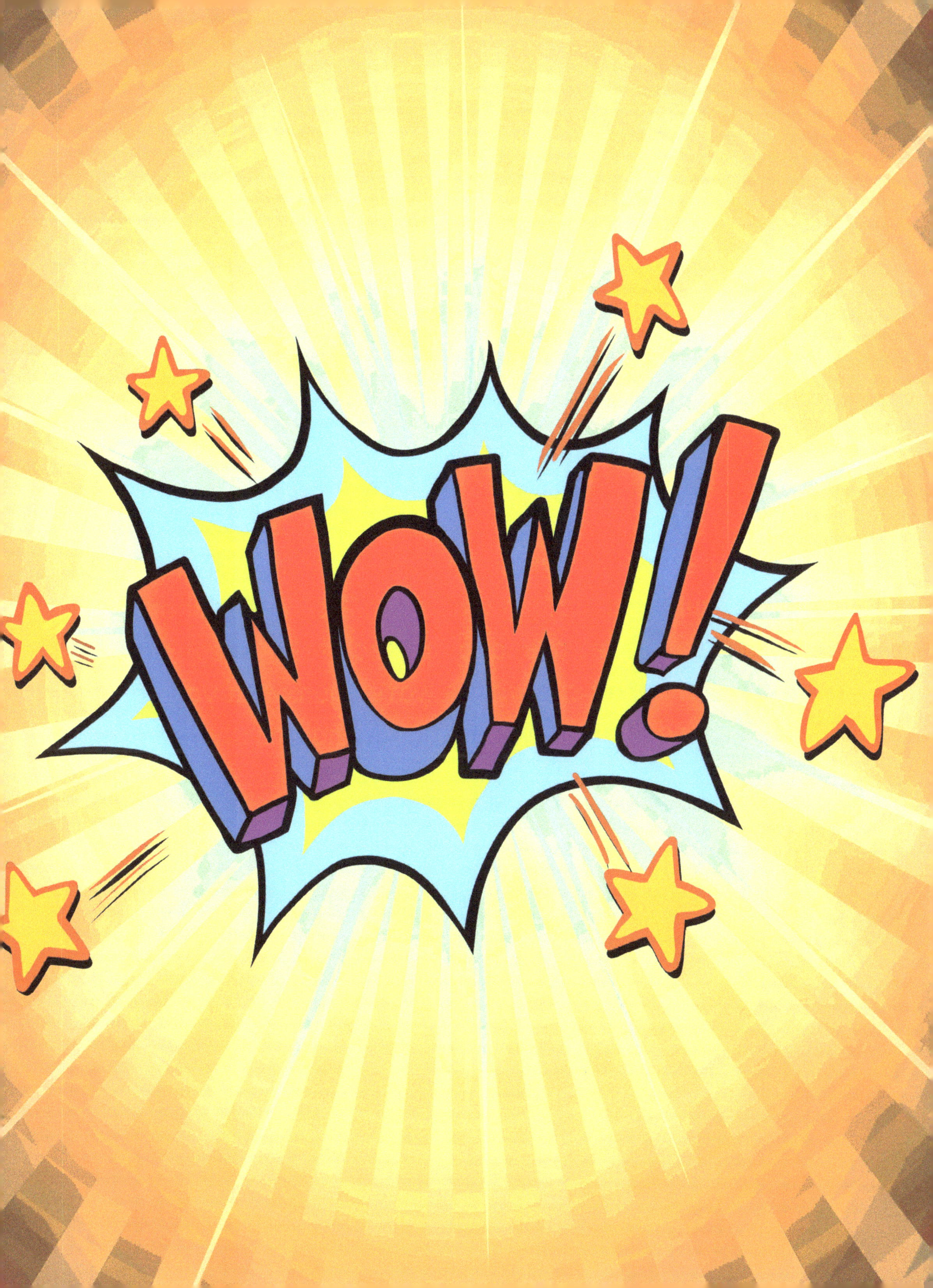
WOW!

And some words rhyme! The word rhyme, rhymes with time, climb, slime, lime, and I'm. You can elaborate, exaggerate, abbreviate, and appreciate! You can also have a ton of fun in the sun with a water gun. And you can take a break and bake a cake or make a shake!

FUN IN THE SUN !

Some of my favorite words are:
Nevertheless, Aqua, Robust, Gibberish, Yikes, Incognito,
Doodle, Abyss, Cornucopia, Melancholy, Thicket,
and Crush.

What are some of your favorite words???

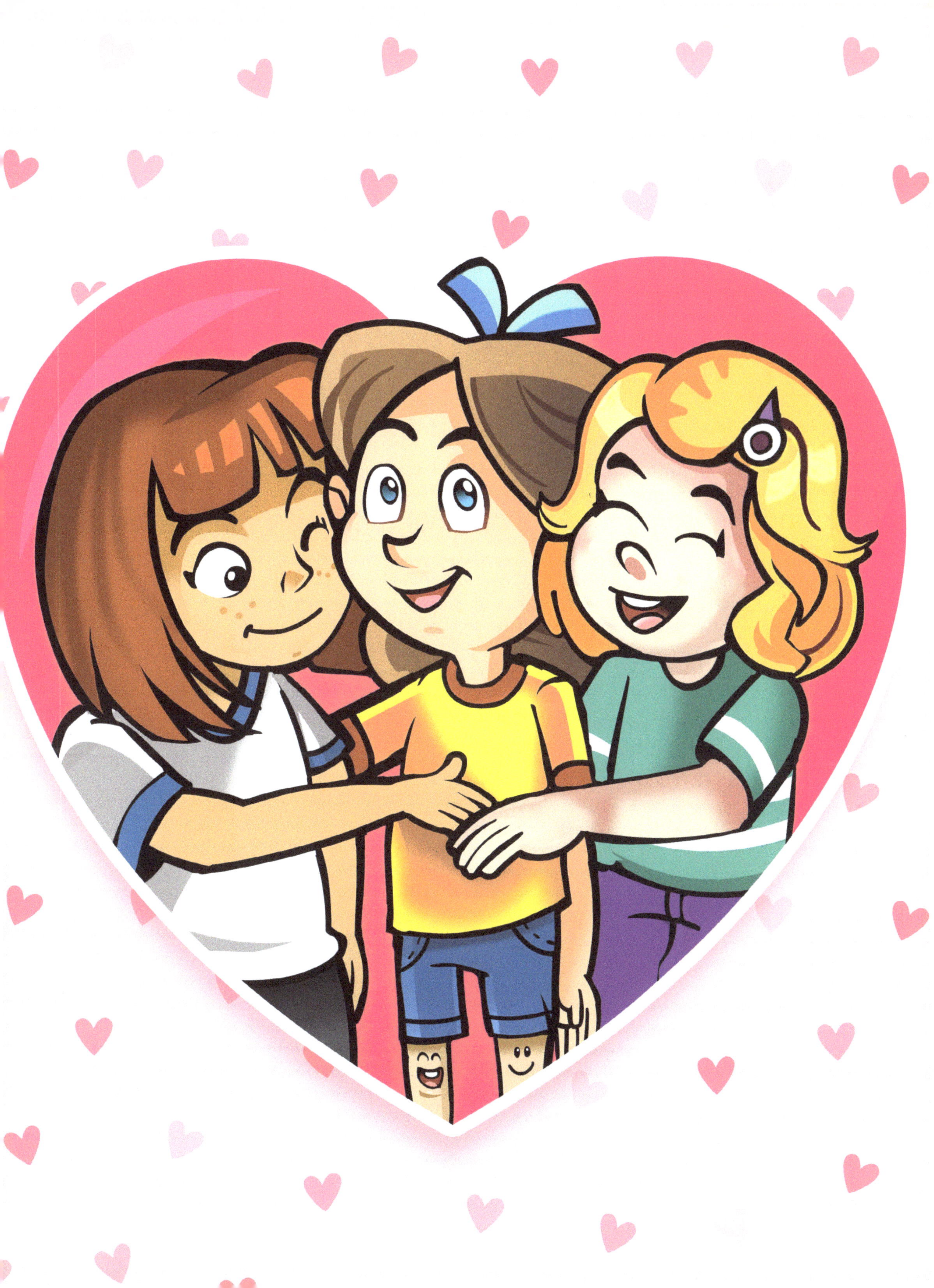

And in closing, the most important words in the whole world are:

I
and
LOVE
and
YOU!

Ingram Content Group UK Ltd.
Milton Keynes UK
UKHW021044190323
418755UK00008B/193